Purpose: Your Passport to Successful Living

Igho Orienru

ROHI Consulting

PURPOSE: YOUR PASSPORT TO SUCCESSFUL LIVING

copyright © **Igho Orienru** 2017
All rights reserved

All rights reserved. No part of this publication may be reproduced, stored in a retrieval system, or transmitted in any form or by any means, electronic, mechanical, photo-copying, recording, or otherwise, without the prior written permission of the author or publisher, with the exception of brief excerpts in magazines, articles, reviews, etc.

Email: orienigho@gmail.com
Tel: +234 (1) 8029767226

ISBN: 978-1977599162

Published by
ROHI Consulting
7 Faramobi Ajike Street
Anthony Village, Lagos

CONTENTS

1. Introduction: Joseph's Breakthrough — 5
2. What is Purpose? — 8
3. The Laws of Purpose — 12
4. The Importance of Purpose — 14
5. Where Can I Find Purpose? — 16
6. The Story of a Manufacturer and his Product — 19
7. How Do I Discover My Purpose? — 23
8. What Is Meditation? — 26
9. Self-Discovery Through Meditation — 29
10. Clue to Self-Discovery: Take Note of Your Dominant Gift — 36
11. General and Specific Purpose for Being Created — 38
12. Service: The Major Activator of Purpose — 44
13. How Useful Are You to Others? — 47
14. Purpose Brings You Success in Life: Testimony of S.B. Fuller — 49

15. Purpose Brings You Success in Life:
    A Natural Launderer & Dry Cleaner
    Discovers Her Purpose   53
16. Thoughts and Declarations   58
17. Fulfilling Your Divine Mandate   61

1

Introduction:
Joseph's Breakthrough

In the history of Israel there is an interesting story of one of their ancestors named Joseph.

At the age of seventeen Joseph dreamt that he would one day be in a position of high authority.

While growing up, Joseph discovered that he was very good at serving people and interpreting dreams, so he gave his best to developing these traits for the benefit of humanity.

One day Pharaoh the King of Egypt had a problem – he had a disturbing dream that none of his wise men could interpret.

Joseph, now a slave prisoner in Egypt, was recommended to Pharaoh as having the ability to interpret dreams. Joseph interpreted the dream and solved the problem, giving the Egyptian king a blueprint that would supply food to the nation during a time of famine.

Joseph was instantly promoted to the position of Prime Minister. Think about it: Joseph woke up that morning a slave boy in prison but slept that night a Prime Minister in a palace.

If I may ask, what brought about this incredible breakthrough for Joseph? It was Purpose. Dearly beloved, the first and most important key to achieving fulfilment in life is Purpose.

Food for Thought

"I am not just here to make a living; I am here to make a difference."
– Helice Bridges

"The greatest and glorious masterpiece of man is to know how to live to Purpose."
– Michael Montaigne

"The greatest tragedy in life is not death, but a life without a purpose."
– Myles Munroe

2

What is Purpose?

Simply put, Purpose is the "why" or reason for the existence of a thing. It is the original intent or desired result for a thing's creation. It is something one has in mind to get or do.

Every life is preceded by Purpose. Every product or design has an intent or motive behind it. It is this intent or motive that gives sense or meaning to its existence; it is the explanation or justification for its being. Purpose is something that is firmly in the mind of an originator or creator as a definite design.

Thus, Purpose is the object or end for which a thing is made or created. Without a definite intention preceding its existence or occurrence, a thing would be a mere accident, a mistake, an embarrassment and an unnecessary complication for which the person responsible would owe others an apology.

Purpose is that issue or activity or hobby that is so strong in your mind that it will be a source of disturbance until it is accomplished.

The extent or degree to which a thing fulfils its purpose is the extent to which it can be judged successful or not. In other words, Purpose is the only valid measure or yardstick for success or failure. Therefore, the value or worth of anything is determined by its purpose and how much of that purpose it fulfils.

For example, money can only be considered successful if it is accepted as legal tender or a medium of exchange. It is not the paper or design that matters, but the capacity to solve financial problems.

This means that true success is not universal but a measure of compliance with purpose. If you bought a television set that produced excellent sound but no pictures, would you say, "Oh, this is an excellent TV set," and place it in your living room instead of returning it for a proper TV set with both sound and pictures? So success is nothing unless it complies with the purpose or intent of a thing.

Life is nothing without purpose. Purpose is the reason we are born and the underlying justification for the gift of life.

3

The Laws of Purpose

1. "Every human being has taken manifestation in physical form to fulfil a divine purpose or intention."

2. "Everyone has a talent, skill or gift, which enables the person to do at least one thing better than anyone else on earth."

According to this law,
1. You have a unique talent and a unique way of expressing the talent. God has an unaccomplished purpose which you are designed to accomplish.

Purpose: Your Passport to Successful Living

You were born an original; refuse to die a photocopy.

2. There is something you were created to do, and you have been equipped to do that thing better than any other person in the world. You are neither a mistake nor a biological accident. Rather, you are an intentional being. Therefore, you are not inferior to anybody, and you must never allow anyone to classify you as substandard.

3. There is a problem God created you to solve. That purpose is why God allowed you to remain alive and well till this moment. God's purpose for your life is for you to make this world a better place than you met it, through the use of the talents and gifts He gave you. So go get that problem solved!

4

The Importance of Purpose

We would do well to remember that –

1. Purpose is more relevant to your success in life than mere goal setting. Here, I am talking of good success, not trial and error.

2. To God, His purpose for your life is more important than anything else. Remember. Proverbs 19:21 says, *"You can make many plans, but the LORD's purpose will prevail."*

3. Purpose is only found in the mind of the creator of a thing. So consult your Creator; He knows everything about you.

4. Purpose is the key to real fulfilment in life. To a great extent, your success in life is tied to your purpose.

5. Purpose preserves, sustains, and protects whoever is living a purposeful life.

6. Purpose, in the sense of your gifts and talents, will always make room for you.

7. Purpose provides you the shortest and safest route to success in life.

5

Where Can I Find Purpose?

It is important to understand that Purpose is never generally revealed from the beginning of a person's life but must be discovered if life is to be meaningful and fulfilling.

One reason why Purpose is hidden is that the purpose of a product precedes the product and no product ever has the privilege of participating in the process by which its purpose is determined. Otherwise we would have come into being armed with the blueprint of our purpose! But it is not that way; we do not have the privilege of knowing the purpose behind our being born. We just get born!

One problem of not knowing our purpose at birth is that we are likely to associate our purpose in life with the prevalent circumstances and social conditions in which we find ourselves.

This is further complicated by the fact that our parents who are the instruments of our production usually do not have a clue as to our purpose beyond their biological and sociological involvements in our being born.

Of course, the purpose or intent of a thing does not lie within the discretion of the instrument by which it is made, but with the maker. While our parents constitute the instruments by which we are fashioned and nurtured or the vehicle of delivery, they are the work tools of a higher hand which designed our destinies even before we drew our first breath.

6

The Story of a Manufacturer and his Product

One day a man I shall call Mr. Brown visited a car shop to buy a car with his hard-earned income.

After inspecting several products, he chose a car made by Ford Motors. Mr. Brown settled the price with the car dealer, issued a cheque for the amount, and was handed the keys and particulars of the car.

Happy that he had fully paid for his first car, Mr. Brown drove home, and thereafter, going to work, visiting friends, relations, and any place of interest, was an exciting cruise for him.

Sometime later he set off on a journey out of town, but on the highway the car developed a fault and Mr. Brown just managed to veer off the road before the car came to a final halt.

Fortunately, there were no vehicles near Mr. Brown's car when the fault developed or there might have been a serious accident. It was a very sad Mr. Brown who alighted from the car; he had no clue what the fault could be and the meeting out of town was a crucial one.

As he stood despondent by his car

watching streams of fast-moving vehicles, a car suddenly pulled up. A stranger emerged from the car and asked him to open the bonnet of his car.

The stranger rolled up his shirt sleeves and set confidently to work on the engine, and in a matter of minutes the car was fixed. Without a word the stranger re-entered his car and was about to drive off when Mr. Brown stopped him.

"Who are you?" he demanded, amazed at the expertise of a man who had done wonders without charging a dime.

The stranger smiled. "What make is your car?"

"A Ford," replied Mr. Brown.

"I am Henry Ford," said the stranger.

"I manufactured your car. That's how I knew exactly how to correct the fault without explanations from you."

God is your manufacturer. Consult him about your life's purpose in the place of quietness and meditation. He will surely fix you up free of charge without delay.

7

How Do I Discover My Purpose?

You would have started on the journey of unravelling the purpose of your existence when you ask questions like:
- Why did God create me?
- Why was I born?
- Why am I the way I am?
- Why did I wake up this morning?
- Why did God allow me to see today?

- Why do I love the things I love and hate the things I hate?
- How do I discover my life's purpose and begin to live it?
- Where do I want to get to in life and how do I get there?

Such questions must become a passion in your heart if answers are to come.

They must be asked solemnly and with confidence in the place of quiet meditation and communion with your Maker. Meditation is a prerequisite for achieving real success in this world.

"This Book of the Law shall not depart from your mouth, but you shall MEDITATE in it day and night, that you may observe to do according to all that

is written in it. For then you will make your way prosperous, and then you will have good success" Joshua 1:8

"The sovereign LORD, the Holy One of Israel, says, "Only in returning to Me and waiting for me will you be saved. In QUIETNESS and confidence is your strength" Isaiah 30:15

"I will guide you along the best pathway for your life. I will advise you and watch over you" Psalm 32:8

8

What is Meditation?

The word "meditation" is from a Latin root, which means "to receive healing." We all need to be in a state where we can receive healing from the confusing circumstances of this world.

Meditation also means to be engaged in deep and serious thought. This includes reflecting quietly on the Creator. In the place of meditation, you are to reflect on Bible Scriptures that are relevant to the knowledge you need, the people whose lives inspire you, the traits you admire in them and how they affect or relate to you.

In the place of meditation, you quietly reflect on yourself in all your hues and shades. It is in the place of meditation that you get clear directives about your life and discover why you were born.

It is here that you learn to separate self from the changing moods of the mind and receive guidance for your life. This is where you find purpose.

Meditation is done in quietness. There must be silence within and around you. It is with discipline, focus, doggedness, patience and absolute dependence on God's strength and direction in the place of meditation that you will succeed in excavating the gold that lies hidden within you.

Essence of Meditation

Get inspired by your Creator and express your discovered purpose for the benefit of mankind. Celebrate your difference, because it is your difference that will attract people to you and make them honour and reward you.

"He who thinks far goes far."
– Belgian proverb

9

Self-Discovery Through Meditation

After achieving quietness within and without, you will need to reflect on some questions in order to ascertain your Strengths, Weaknesses, Opportunities, and Threats in an analysis known as SWOT.

Jot down your answers, develop actions plans, and start executing them. The questions are stated under these heads:

Natural Proficiency

What do I enjoy doing, which I can do well and easily, but which others might find difficult or boring? (Sometimes what we call a hobby is really our calling.)

Motivation

If I had all the time and money in the world, what dream or occupation would most motivate me? What sphere of influence sets me on fire and consumes me? (Our passion or burning desire may be our calling!)

Satisfaction

From what activities do I derive a satisfaction that goes far beyond monetary gain?

Service

If I had all the money in the world, what would I want to do for the betterment of others? What makes me angry and concerned? What are those societal challenges that I cannot get out of my head? (You may be called to confront those problems with your talents, resources and time.)

A detailed analysis of the answers to these questions will go a long way in helping you to recognize your **strengths**, and your strengths are a good pointer to what career or business you should pursue.

What to Avoid

What are those activities you are

neither excited about nor proficient in doing?

- He who wastes his time wastes his life.
- What you pay attention to grows!
- Not everything that takes your time needs your time.

It is important that you identify activities that represent your **weaknesses** and refrain from doing them. It they are things that must be done, you should delegate or outsource them. If you don't, they may prevent you from maximizing your God-given talents and achieving your goals.

What to Go for

- What is lacking in your community

that you could use your naturally-endowed talents to provide and thereby make a positive impact on humanity?

- How can you use your talents to gain eternal as well as financial rewards while blessing and helping humanity?

Trying to find answers to these two questions will help you discover opportunities that come your way daily so you can benefit from them.

Prevention
- What are the challenges that you may likely come across?

- What are your plans to overcome these challenges?

Research and counsel from experts, who may include lawyers, insurers, accountants and tax authorities, could help mitigate seen and unforeseen risks that could be **threats** in the pursuit of your purpose.

Sphere of Influence

Which sphere of influence are you mandated to take for the Creator?

There are seven areas or spheres of influence that describe society, and you are empowered and mandated by your Creator to rule and reign with the keys of exercising dominance in at least one of these spheres.

The spheres are:

i/ Governance (government and politics);

ii/ Economy (business and finance);

iii/ Education (knowledge acquisition and transfer);

iv/ Family (social and health);

v/ Religion (raising balanced leaders);

vi/ Celebration (art, culture, entertainment, and sports);

vii/ Media (upholding and propagating truth)

10

Clue to Self-Discovery: Take Note of Your Dominant Gift

By close observation, you will notice a natural pull and attraction towards certain areas of interest. Activities in these areas so engross you that you lose track of time.

Opportunities to engage in these activities give you a level of joy and satisfaction more valuable than monetary gain. This is a clue to discovering your dominant gift.

Purpose: Your Passport to Successful Living

Activities that utilize your dominant gift always give you satisfaction far beyond monetary value.

Recognize your dominant gift and maximize its use by developing it and praying for clarity and specific directions concerning it.

It is in doing this that you will achieve breakthroughs, attain greatness, and fulfil purpose.

11

General and Specific Purpose for Being Created

It must be understood that there is a general as well as a specific purpose why we were created.

General Purpose

Revelation chapter 4 verse 11 says:
Thou art worthy, O Lord, to receive glory and honour and power: for thou hast created all things, and for thy pleasure they are and were created.

All things were created by God for

His own pleasure. That is, the pleasure of God is the underlying purpose of all of creation.

A simple way of describing the things that give God pleasure is to look at nature in its pristine state. Imagine the sheer force, energy and awesomeness of the ocean!

Or the magnificence and beauty of the rising and setting sun! Consider the colourful butterflies as they dance in flight from nectar to nectar among finely petalled flowers.

Or the birds that sing, the trees that sway, the streams that whisper through the woods and the innocent, unburdened laughter of little children; then you will know that God's pleasure is sweet!

Like the gentle breeze that caresses the weary face. Like the taste or the feel of water on the parched tongue. Like the stretch of sand at the seashore, white and ever drinking of the overflow of surging waters.

Imagine the goodness of a God that created beauty and the eyes to see it; the tongue that discerns taste and the nose that perceives smell.

He made the sweet and the bitter, the beautiful and the ugly, the great and the small in order that we may appreciate the difference.

This God must be good in ways that we cannot tell. It is His pleasure that designed the ecosystem where the tiniest bits of creation support, in delicate balance, the existence of the massive hulks of creation. A system where nothing is too small and nothing is too big; where everything matters.

It is for this pleasure that He created man in His own image and likeness and gave him dominion over the works of His hand.

Specific Purpose

Genesis chapter 1 verses 26 to 28 read as follows:

26 And God said, Let us make man in our image, after our likeness: and let them have dominion over the fish of the sea, and over the fowl of the air, and over the cattle, and over all the earth, and over every creeping thing that creepeth upon the earth.

27 So God created man in his own image, in the image of God created he him; male and female created he them.

28 And God blessed them, and God said unto them, Be fruitful, and multiply, and replenish the earth, and subdue it: and have dominion over the fish of the sea, and over the fowl of the air, and over every living thing that moveth upon the earth.

From the above text we see that God declared your purpose before you were created.

Man, you were born to be fruitful, to multiply, replenish the earth, subdue, and have dominion and controlling influence over everything created by God apart from fellow humans.

To achieve this purpose, God made you in His image and likeness. You were not created to be under the whiplash of circumstances but to take charge and be in control of a specific sphere of influence.

That is your specific purpose! Discover your sphere of influence and start running with it!

Whenever man fulfils this purpose (general and specific), God is pleased.

12

Service: The Major Activator of Purpose

The Scriptures read as follows in Mark chapter 10 verses 42 to 45 (NLT):

42. So Jesus called them together and said, 'You know that in this world kings are tyrants, and officials lord it over the people beneath them.

43. But among you it should be quite different. Whoever wants to be a leader among you must be your servant,

44. and whoever wants to be first must be the slave of all.

45. For even I, the Son of Man, came here to serve others, and to give my life as a ransom for many.

Service is the act of rendering a task satisfactorily to another person. It is work undertaken according to the instructions of the person to whom it is rendered.

Service is the helpful act of being useful to others. Until we come to the point in our lives when we realize that life is about serving others, we will never come close to our purpose in life.

Every reward that was ever made was for a problem solved or a service rendered.

Any gift given to anyone is to be used for the benefit of others. Light does not shine for itself. The tree does not eat its own fruit, nor the vine its own wine. The spring does not drink its own water.

No musician, artiste, athlete, writer or entertainer or manufacturer is ever fulfilled to produce and consume his own product.

Purpose is found only in what we can give. This is what qualifies us to receive in order to be able to give again.

13

How Useful Are You to Others?

It is a clear fact that you are created to serve others with your gifts and talents.

That is, you are to cheerfully render service to your fellow human beings, using purpose to better their lots here on earth.

Purpose does not ask, "What is in it for me?" The only question a man or woman of purpose should ask is, "How can I be of help to all the people I'll come across today?"

As a person of purpose, your focus must remain, "How can I always be of service to humanity today?" Your obedience is only complete in the place of service.

This is not just a humanitarian position. It is the key to success and relevance; for it is only in adding value to others that we are valued by others.

Success is only a measure of relevance, and relevance is only a measure of how you affect others or what you mean to them. Service is the doorway to purpose.

14

Purpose Brings You Success in Life: Testimony of S.B. Fuller

The success story of S.B. Fuller is legendary. He was one of seven children born to a black farmer in Louisiana in the United States of America.

By the age of five, he had started work and by the time he was nine, he was driving mules.

This was not unusual because the children of most farmers started earning their keep early. These black farmers had long ago accepted poverty as their portion in life and asked for no more. Their condition was so bad and bleak that S.B. Fuller's father could not entertain the dream of being wealthy.

In the midst of that dark, miserable world of poverty was a beacon of light: Fuller's mother was a dreamer. She refused to accept poverty.

She believed it was possible for one to step out of the slums and stand with people who mattered. She began to feed her young son's brain with dreams of greatness.

She explained to him that they were poor simply because none of them had ever developed a desire to be anything else. Fuller then developed a burning desire to be rich.

As soon as he was old enough, he began to sell soap from door to door, until he made enough money to buy out the company that used to supply him.

When asked years later the secret of his success, he answered in terms of his mother's motivating statement made so many years earlier:

We are poor – not because of God. We are poor because father has never developed a desire to become rich. No one in our family has ever developed a desire to be anything else.

It was this statement that made young S.B. Fuller determined to stand out in the crowd, to leave the ranks of faceless farmers and live a life of purpose.

And he succeeded!

No man has ever made it by accident. The Hall of Fame is not for wayfarers.

You must set out purposely in your quest to be somebody or to make this world a better place than you met it.

You shall succeed in Jesus' Name!

15

Purpose Brings You Success in Life: A Natural Launderer & Dry Cleaner Discovers Her Purpose

For several years a lady in Lagos, Nigeria, whom I shall call Npio, tried her hands at different things, including paid employment, contract work, and trading, but couldn't find fulfilment.

While searching for something profitable and fulfilling to do which had flexible hours to enable her have enough time for her family, she sought the assistance of a consultant (the author of this book).

She was taken through a self-assessment exercise called *Am I in the Right Work?* This is an exercise similar to the *Personal SWOT Analysis* recommended in the "Self-Discovery Through Meditation" section of this book.

Npio carefully completed the exercise and also had some personal coaching sessions with her consultant.

In the process she discovered a talent she had possessed from childhood which she could convert to commercial use for the benefit of others and herself.

This natural talent was the ability to help people launder and dry clean their clothes. *"He who thinks far goes far."*

With this discovery, Npio put aside her tertiary education certificates and set about acquiring the skills needed to become a professional launderer and dry cleaner, which she became in record time.

Advised by her consultant, she adopted the "Modelling Technique" of skill acquisition. That is, Npio learnt the laundry and dry-cleaning trade from an experienced one-time staff member of a defunct dry cleaning company, mainly to learn the reasons for the company's closure as a pre-emptive strategy.

Then Npio took further training from a small dry-cleaning firm to learn what it takes to survive as a dry cleaner.

Then she had a stint with a leading dry-cleaning company in Lagos to gain the secret of becoming a reputable and successful dry cleaner.

Finally, Npio did apprenticeship with a lady dry cleaner whose business was run from home and who also provided office collection and delivery services.

For Npio, like the woman, planned to start her dry-cleaning business from home – starting small but ending big.

Within three years Npio's operation had grown from a small home business to an ultra-modern establishment with top-range machines and staff, located in an enviable residential area of Lagos.

What is Npio's secret? Npio is not just the owner of a dry-cleaning firm but is also a born dry cleaner. Her search for what to do is over.

She is now a proud employer of labour, positively contributing to the improvement of the Nigerian economy.

"A man who qualifies himself well for his calling never fails of employment."
— Thomas Jefferson

16

Thoughts and Declarations

Listed below are some thoughts worth pondering on and some declarations worth making.

Thoughts to Ponder

- The starting point of all achievements is definiteness of purpose.
- True Success is not universal; it is only a measure of compliance with purpose.
- The big issue of life is to unravel the purpose behind being born and to fulfil it.

- Purpose does not lie within the discretion of the tool or instrument, but with the maker.
- Time and life are meaningless without purpose.
- The price tag you place on your head will determine the value people will place on you.

My Purpose Declaration

- I will consult my Creator to discover the real me. To achieve this, I will spend time in meditative silence each day – thirty minutes in the morning and thirty minutes at night before going to bed.
- I will work hard to discover, develop and express my unique talents for the benefit of mankind.

- As I express my unique talents, I shall enjoy being carried to timeless consciousness.
- I resolve to give to everyone I meet today a dose of love, joy, peace, satisfaction, and happiness.
- I will do my best to ensure that I exploit my potential to the maximum in serving humanity on a daily basis.
- I will ask myself this question daily: "How am I best suited to serve and help humanity today?"
- I shall answer this question and do as I have answered, serving humanity.

SO HELP ME GOD!

17

FULFILLING YOUR DIVINE MANDATE

As stated earlier, there are seven areas or spheres of influence that describe society, and you are empowered and mandated by your Creator to rule and reign with the keys of dominance in at least one of these spheres.

The following Scriptures bear this out: Gen 1:27-28; Gen 9:1-2; Luke 4:18; Luke 10:19.

Laid out on the next page is a table listing out each of the spheres and the issues that are prevalent to each sphere, as well as the competencies required to reign and have dominance in the spheres, and their benefits to Christ's Kingdom.

Once you have identified your sphere or spheres, this table should be used as a guide to direct you in fulfilling your purpose and becoming a blessing and solution provider to your generation and posterity.

Purpose: Your Passport to Successful Living

S/N	Sphere or Mountain of Society	Prevalent Issues in Each Sphere or Mountain	Disciples to be Developed and Deployed	Benefits to Christ's Kingdom
1	Governance (Government/ Politics)	• Corruption • Greed • Selfishness • Pride • Lack of leadership skills	Marketplace Apostles with spiritual fortitude, resilience, and leadership skills to lead special interest groups.	All **POWER** will finally belong to Jesus the Christ.
2	Economy (Business/ Finance)	• Corruption • Poor business & financial management skills	Prophets and leaders like Joseph to establish Godly principles in the marketplace.	All **RICHES** will finally belong to Jesus the Christ.
3	Education (Knowledge acquisition/ transfer)	• Secular humanism • Rejection of God's value system	Teachers who are grounded in the word of God and who apply the word to effectively transfer knowledge.	All **WISDOM** will finally belong to Jesus the Christ.

4	Family (Values/Social/ Health)	•Dysfunctional & delinquent children •Divorce •Illnesses etc.	Pastors with caring hearts to bind up broken families and refocus families on God.	All **STRENGTH** will finally belong to Jesus the Christ.
5	Religion (raising balanced leaders)	•Denominationalism • Sectarianism • The inability to handle complex societal issues	Priests who will raise sons and daughters to serve as kings and priests in the seven spheres of society.	All **HONOUR** will finally belong to Jesus the Christ.
6	Celebration (Art, Culture, Entertainment, Sports)	• Seduction • Lust • Pornography • Illegality	Evangelists and prophets who will use music, drama, sports and entertainment to disseminate the Gospel uncompromisingly.	All **GLORY** will finally belong to Jesus the Christ.
7	Media (upholding/ propagating truth)	• News heavily laced with lies • Distortion • Blackmail • Fear • Terror	Evangelists who will tell the truth in the context of God's perspective.	All **BLESSINGS** will finally belong to Jesus the Christ.

*Source: The Grand Design by Prof Vincent Anigbogu and Pst Sunday Adelaja

Conclusion

Let me congratulate you for taking your time to read this book to the end. I trust you have also done the recommended exercises? If not, please go back and do them and begin to practise the principles you have learnt.

Dearly beloved, the journey of purpose discovery and fulfilment is a lifetime journey. Now that you have started it, please do not ever stop. Keep at it because success lies in consistency.

Congratulations!

www.ingramcontent.com/pod-product-compliance
Lightning Source LLC
Chambersburg PA
CBHW030504220526
45464CB00006B/2645